20TH CENTURY MEDIA

20s & 30s

ENTERTAINMENT FOR ALL

Please visit our web site at: www.garethstevens.com
For a free color catalog describing Gareth Stevens Publishing's
list of high-quality books and multimedia programs, call
1-800-542-2595 (USA) or 1-800-387-3178 (Canada).
Gareth Stevens Publishing's fax: (414) 332-3567.

Library of Congress Cataloging-in-Publication Data

Parker, Steve.
    20th century media / by Steve Parker.
        v. cm.
    Includes bibliographical references and index.
    Contents: [1] 1900–20: print to pictures.   [2] 20s & 30s: entertainment for all.
[3] 40s & 50s: power and persuasion.   [4] 1960s: the Satellite Age.   [5] 70s & 80s:
global technology.   [6] 1990s: electronic media.
    ISBN 0-8368-3182-9 (v. 1: lib. bdg.) — ISBN 0-8368-3183-7 (v. 2: lib. bdg.) —
ISBN 0-8368-3184-5 (v. 3: lib. bdg.) — ISBN 0-8368-3185-3 (v. 4: lib. bdg.) —
ISBN 0-8368-3186-1 (v. 5: lib. bdg.) — ISBN 0-8368-3187-X (v. 6: lib. bdg.)
    1. Mass media—History—20th century—Juvenile literature.   [1. Mass
media—History—20th century.]   I. Title: Twentieth century media.   II. Title.
P91.2.P37   2002
302.23'09'04—dc21   2002022556

This North American edition first published in 2002 by
Gareth Stevens Publishing
A World Almanac Education Group Company
330 West Olive Street, Suite 100
Milwaukee, Wisconsin 53212 USA

Original edition © 2002 by David West Children's Books. First published in Great Britain
in 2002 by Heinemann Library, Halley Court, Jordan Hill, Oxford OX2 8EJ, a division of Reed
Educational and Professional Publishing Limited. This U.S. edition © 2002 by Gareth Stevens, Inc.
Additional end matter © 2002 by Gareth Stevens, Inc.

Designer: Rob Shone
Editor: James Pickering
Picture Research: Carrie Haines

Gareth Stevens Editor: Dorothy L. Gibbs

Photo Credits:
Abbreviations: (t) top, (m) middle, (b) bottom, (l) left, (r) right

The Advertising Archive Ltd.: page 13(br).
AKG: pages 20-21.
The Art Archive: pages 4(mr), 11(tr), 29(br); British Library: page 29(bl); Eileen Tweedy: page 5(bl).
Bell Laboratories: page 23(r).
Corbis Stock Market: cover (all).
The Culture Archive: pages 4(bl), 23(ml).
Mary Evans Picture Library: pages 3, 5(br), 6(tr), 7(tr), 10(tr), 16(br), 21(bl), 22(tr), 24(tr), 24-25, 25(tr),
    26 (bl, m), 27(l).
Hulton Archive: pages 9(tr, br), 12(tr), 12-13(b), 14(all), 15(tl, mr), 16(l), 17(t), 22(bl), 25(m), 26(tr), 28(b).
The Kobal Collection: pages 4(br), 18(both), 19(br), 20(both).
Popperfoto: pages 5(t), 6(bl), 6-7, 7(br), 8(both), 9(ml), 10(bl, br), 11(l, br), 12-13(t), 13(tr), 17(ml, mr),
    18-19, 19(tr), 21(br), 22(m), 24(b), 26(ml), 28(t), 29(tr).
Reader's Digest: page 27(br); Bradford Bachrach: page 27(bm-b); Fabian Bachrach: page 27(bm-t).

Printed in the United States of America

1 2 3 4 5 6 7 8 9 06 05 04 03 02

20TH CENTURY MEDIA

20s & 30s

ENTERTAINMENT FOR ALL

Steve Parker

Gareth Stevens Publishing
A WORLD ALMANAC EDUCATION GROUP COMPANY

CONTENTS

In 1936, Penguin Books started a new publishing trend — paperbacks. Unlike books with hard covers, paperbacks were inexpensive enough for almost anyone to buy.

Radio sets brought a new world of listening pleasure directly into people's homes. RCA established the Radiola name in 1921. This advertisement is from 1928.

Until 1927, movies were silent, with only musical accompaniment. Then, singer-actor Al Jolson amazed the world by speaking directly from the screen. "Talkies" had arrived.

INSTANT MEDIA

We find out what happens in the world through the media. They provide news, knowledge, and entertainment. We have many forms of media today, the newest being the Internet. In 1920, forms of media were fewer. Newspapers were the main medium for spreading news. Radio was just starting up. Television did not exist. Cinema was established, but movies were silent — no sound came directly from the screen.

The next twenty years brought huge changes. By 1940, radio offered instant news, movies had sound, and television sets were creeping into homes. Technology was racing forward, and media businesses boomed. Some things, sadly, did not change. The world was again at war.

When World War II broke out in 1939, the media played a greater role than ever before in spreading news and shaping public opinion.

Some people feared that radio and television might become too powerful. Would these media lull listeners and viewers into just sitting around being told what to think and keep them from having any views of their own?

From about 1920, magazines expanded to carry a mix of news reports, in-depth analyses of events, features, and fiction. Fortune was founded in 1930.

GREATEST SHOW ON EARTH

Every four years, the Olympic Games, probably the world's greatest sports event, brings together athletes of all nations in peace and harmony. Several times, unfortunately, media coverage of the Olympics has been used for less peaceful purposes.

MEDIA GAMES

A world event like the Olympics creates massive public interest and media coverage. On occasion, both have been "hijacked" by a cause that is not connected with the Olympics, or even with sports. The 1936 Olympic Games were held in Berlin, Germany, when the German nation was controlled by Adolf Hitler's Nazi movement.

Nazis glorified strength, physical prowess, and discipline.

Jesse Owens beat his rivals in the 100-meter-sprint final at the 1936 Olympic Games.

MEDIA OPPORTUNITY

Millions of people were reading about the Olympics in newspapers and magazines, listening on radios, and watching newsreel films. Hitler saw an ideal opportunity to tell the world about Nazi supremacy. Germany had used every possible means, including all the latest scientific advancements and training methods, to build its athletic teams. Its goal was to dominate the Games and show how powerful and successful the Nazi movement had become.

Adolf Hitler (fifth from left) and other Nazi officials gave a raised-arm salute at the opening ceremony of the 1936 Olympic Games. The salute had nothing to do with the Games, but it appeared in photographs and newsreel films all over the world.

ARYANS IN THE MEDIA

Nazis believed in the future of the Aryan race. Aryans were strong, fit, intelligent German people who were destined to rule others, who followed their leader without question and would die for him, and who were white. The Germans used books, newspapers, films, works of art, and other media to spread the idea of Aryan greatness.

German artist Wolf Willrich painted this picture-perfect Aryan family.

Unlike Nazi leader Adolf Hitler, the people of Germany cheered for Olympic champion Jesse Owens.

AN ANGRY EXIT

Although Germany won more medals than any other nation in the 1936 Olympics, Hitler's racist dreams of supremacy backfired. Through the media, the world watched U. S. athlete Jesse Owens become the undisputed star of the Games. Owens won four gold medals, one each for the 100- and 200-meter sprints, one for the long jump, and one as a member of the 400-meter relay team. Furious that a black athlete beat the best of his white-only Aryan team, Hitler stormed out of the stadium.

RADIO'S GOLDEN AGE

During World War I (1914–1918), radio broadcasting by the public was banned in many countries so it would not interfere with radio's secret use by the military. Nevertheless, the technology of radio leaped ahead.

READY TO GROW

By 1920, wartime broadcasting bans were being lifted, and radio was ready to spread like wildfire. Many small stations sprang up, especially in the United States and Britain. One of the first station licenses in the United States went to Dr. Frank Conrad, a Westinghouse engineer, for Radio KDKA in East Pittsburgh. KDKA's first broadcast brought updated news of the 1920 presidential election faster than any newspaper.

Broadcasting House, in Central London, became the home of BBC Radio in 1932. This prestigious office building was a symbol of radio's powerful media status.

John Reith (1889–1971), the first director-general of the BBC, set very high standards in all areas of radio broadcasting. He served until 1938.

COMMERCIAL BOOM

New York radio station WEAF, established in 1922 by U. S. corporation AT&T, brought a new trend to radio — commercials. The first commercial was a ten-minute speech promoting the Queensborough Corporation, a real estate business. In 1923, WEAF made an incredible $150,000 profit. Radio "business" was booming.

William Paley (1901–1990) developed U. S. radio network CBS into a multi-million-dollar business. He was the chairman of CBS until 1946.

Guglielmo Marconi (1874–1937), who invented the first practical radio, also set up successful radio businesses. RCA purchased the American Marconi Company in 1919.

A DIFFERENT APPROACH

Radio in Britain developed in a different direction. The British Broadcasting Corporation (BBC) began as a private enterprise with a news bulletin from Marconi House in The Strand, London, on November 14, 1922. In 1927, the BBC received a charter from the British government allowing it to become totally independent. The BBC was supposed "to educate, to entertain, and to inform." It was also to remain unaffected by pressure from politicians, governments, and businesses and receive no money from commercials.

NETWORK RIVALS

Radio Corporation of America (RCA) started business as a radio technology company. It set up the National Broadcasting Company (NBC), its broadcasting network, in 1926, under general manager David Sarnoff (1891–1971). NBC's rival, the Columbia Broadcasting System (CBS), was founded in 1927 and grew rapidly under William Paley.

Reading the news, in 1935

HOW RADIO WORKS

Radio waves are made of both electrical and magnetic energy. The invisible waves are sent out, or broadcasted, by a transmitter, from a wire called an aerial, and are picked up by a receiver, which is the radio set.

MAKING WAVES

Radio uses a basic carrier wave that is altered, or modulated, to convey information in the form of a pattern or code. The first broadcasts used AM waves, in which the amplitude, or height, of the waves is altered. By 1933, U. S. radio engineer Edwin Armstrong had invented FM waves, in which the frequency, or number of waves per second, is modulated. FM produced clearer sounds and was less affected by weather.

Transmitter

Radio wave

Basic carrier wave

AM (amplitude modulated) wave

FM (frequency modulated) wave

FAST AS LIGHT

Radio waves are similar to light waves and travel just as quickly. Because they are largely unaffected by day or night, rain or clouds, they are ideal for carrying information almost instantly. To broadcast radio waves over greater distances, scientists in the 1920s developed more powerful transmitters from long aerial wires on tall poles.

Smaller aerial poles appeared on houses to pick up the radio waves and feed them to the receiver — the radio set.

Radio relay stations picked up broadcasts from far away, boosted their strength, and sent them onward.

THE "RADIO MUSIC BOX"

In 1916, David Sarnoff, then employed by American Marconi, suggested that radio could be a major medium for news and entertainment. He envisioned speech and music brought into every home through a simple "Radio Music Box." By 1925, sales of these boxes, or radio sets, were skyrocketing. The two main kinds of radios were the crystal set and the valve set. The crystal set needed little or no electricity but produced only enough volume for headphones. The electronic triode valves of the valve set produced signals strong enough to drive a loudspeaker but needed a powerful electricity supply.

For extra volume, this RadiAir receiver (1926) had five valves and a horn-shaped speaker.

In 1922, the BTH receiver was one of the world's smallest, and it did not need a long aerial wire.

THE FIGHTS HEARD LIVE!

In 1920, most sports fans had to read about events in the next day's newspaper. Radio brought sports news and commentary as the events happened. One of the first big events heard live was the world heavyweight boxing championship between Jack Dempsey and George Carpenter on July 2, 1921. This fight was also the first million-dollar boxing event.

"Dempsey has a knockout in the fourth round!"

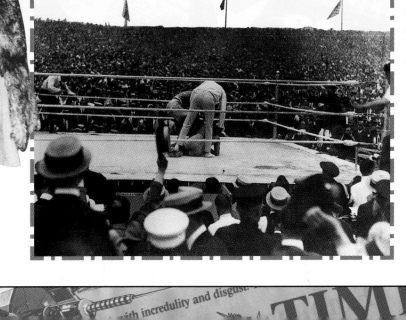

FEEDING THE AIRWAVES

During radio's "Golden Age," which lasted from the 1920s until the 1950s, the range of programs expanded from mostly news and music to include current affairs, sports, drama, comedy, and light entertainment.

NONSTOP NEWS

One of the great events during radio's early years was the first solo transatlantic flight by U. S. aviator Charles Lindbergh, in 1927. Such international news usually had to be "wired" by telegraph for reporting in newspapers. For this event, however, the world sat by their radios, waiting for news about the lone flier, who, oddly enough, did not have a radio in his aircraft. When the 33-hour trip ended, listeners heard the news of Lindbergh's Paris landing — live! — and were celebrating a new national hero well before newspapers could print the story.

THE RATINGS

In commercial radio, advertising was priced according to the popularity of the program. In 1930, Crossley, Inc., in the United States, produced the first program ratings based on official estimated numbers of listeners. NBC's *Amos 'n' Andy* was the most popular show.

The fast-talking, breathless, deadpan style of journalist-commentator Walter Winchell (1897–1972) influenced many announcers. His radio audience reached 20 million.

White comedians Freeman Gosden (right) and Charles Correll (left) were the creators and voices of black radio stars Amos and Andy.

On October 30, 1938, Orson Welles broadcasted the H. G. Wells story The War of the Worlds as a Halloween spoof, but a million panicked Americans believed Martians were really invading.

When the giant passenger airship Hindenberg *exploded in New Jersey, in May 1937, radio news announcers were overwhelmed and reduced to tears.*

FAMILIAR VOICES

Many early radio stars became known by their catchphrases. U. S. journalist Walter Winchell wrote newspaper gossip columns and, in 1932, adapted the idea for radio. He began each Sunday-night, network program with "Good evening, Mr. and Mrs. America and all the ships at sea." Comedy stars Jack Benny, George Burns, and Gracie Allen were also familiar voices.

THE FIRST "SOAPS"

Long-running drama serials, called "soap operas," had their origins on radio in the late 1920s. Many people listened to the radio at home during the day, while doing housework. Makers of soaps, polishes, and other cleaning products recognized this audience and began to advertise. Soon, they were sponsoring entire programs.

A newspaper version of a soap ad

IVORY SOAP

TV'S FALSE START

By the early 1920s, radio was sending speech, music, and many other sounds instantly, even over great distances. Radio was a new, exciting, and rapidly expanding medium, but inventors were already wondering if radio waves could carry moving pictures, too.

In John Logie Baird's 1926 "wireless vision" transmissions, pictures sent by radio waves had a ghostly appearance. Shown at the rate of ten per second, the pictures merged, creating the impression of movement.

John Logie Baird looks down a picture tube at the Nipkow scanning disk on one of his early pieces of "television" equipment.

EARLY TESTS

Still photographs were first sent as coded patterns of radio waves from New York to London in 1924. It was a fast way to send pictures for newspapers. Radio, however, could broadcast sounds "live" and continuously, as they happened. The aim was to do the same with pictures.

THE SPINNING DISK

In 1922, Scottish electrical engineer John Logie Baird (1888–1946) was already working to improve a system that had been devised by German physicist Paul Nipkow (1860–1940) in the 1880s. Nipkow's system used a fast-rotating "scanning" disk that contained slots or holes. In 1926, Baird sent his first moving images by "wireless vision," or television, a short distance between attic rooms in Soho, London. The face on the dim, fuzzy screen was that of a boy who just happened to be passing by.

THE TV BUSINESS

By 1927, Baird was sending pictures from city to city. The scanning disk was the camera. Baird also worked on color and large-screen television. He even recorded TV programs on disks similar to those used for sound recording. Although his system faded out, Baird helped establish television's huge future as the next big medium.

City-to-city television

In 1926, Baird's pictures had 30 scanned lines. By 1936, the BBC was broadcasting pictures using a Baird system with 240 lines, which made the images sharper and clearer.

John Logie Baird tunes an early "wireless vision" receiver, or TV set. In 1936, the BBC decided to switch to a rival all-electronic version.

IMPROVEMENTS

Baird transmitted televisual pictures from London to Glasgow in 1927 and from London to New York in 1928. In 1929, he began daily, half-hour test broadcasts for the BBC, in London, with both sound and vision carried by radio waves. Baird's success continued for a few more years, but it was a false start. By 1936, all-electronic systems had taken over.

EARLY TELEVISION CAMERA

Spinning Nipkow disk

Bright light

Light shining through hole

Focusing lens

Light reflecting off of object

Gate

Image to transmitter

Photocells detect light spots.

In Baird's system, a disk with slots or holes rotated to let tiny spots of light shine through in fast succession. The spots were aimed to "scan" an object by moving up, down, and across it. Photocells changed the brightness of each spot into a corresponding electrical pulse, which was transmitted to a receiver. The receiver worked in reverse, projecting the moving spots of light onto a screen. Baird's system was limited by wear and tear on its moving parts and the need to adjust the sending and receiving disks with extreme precision.

The image seen on-screen

FLICKERING SCREEN

Today's main medium is television. Life without TV may be difficult to imagine, but television did not exist until the 1920s. It began as an experiment. By the 1930s, it found its way into a few homes, mostly those of the rich and famous. Then, its progress was delayed, partly by World War II (1939–1945). Television started to become more commonplace in the 1950s.

The BBC began all-electronic TV broadcasts in 1936. In 1938, it set up television studios at Alexandra Palace, in North London.

INVISIBLE BEAM

As John Logie Baird worked on his partially mechanical television system, Russian-born American physicist Vladimir Zworykin (1889–1982) was developing a version with no moving parts. Zworykin used an invisible beam of electrons, which are tiny atomic particles. The beam was produced inside a cathode-ray tube, a device that was invented in 1897.

Future TV? A view from 1927

At Alexandra Palace, BBC programs were sent out using an electronic system devised by Marconi-EMI. The pictures had 405 scanned lines, which was both an improvement over John Logie Baird's 240-line system and the world's first high-definition television.

RCA's David Sarnoff invested $50 million in Zworykin's work. Sarnoff saw television as an important new medium — and a profitable one!

Vladimir Zworykin was working at Westinghouse when he developed his electronic television system, in 1923. He called the tube an iconoscope.

OLD TUBE, NEW USE

Zworykin made the front of the tube into a screen. Electrons from a "gun" at the back of the tube hit the inside of the screen, which was coated with dots of a substance called phosphor. The phosphor glowed when the electrons hit it. As the beam moved, or scanned, line by line down the screen, the glowing dots built up pictures. The pictures changed so fast that movement seemed continuous.

THE FUTURE OF TV?

In the late 1920s, with television programs being broadcasted in patchy areas, news of this unusual new medium was spreading — but would TV be a success? The screens of early television receivers were small, dim, and blurry, so viewing hardly seemed worth the bother. Radio sets were much easier to use and offered far more programs.

BROADCASTING BEGINS

In Britain, the Marconi-EMI Television Company was developing similar equipment. It demonstrated test systems in 1932, and the BBC began regular broadcasts in 1936. Still, progress continued to be slow. In 1939, RCA showed U. S. president Franklin D. Roosevelt speaking at the New York World's Fair. The event marked the first presidential television broadcast from the United States.

At THE MOVIES

By 1920, movies had become the main medium for entertainment. With no television yet, and with radio still in its infancy, going to movies was an affordable way for people to escape from daily routines and life's problems.

HOLLYWOOD!

A district called Hollywood, in the northwestern section of Los Angeles, California, ruled the American movie business. The first movie studio there was built in 1911, and by 1920, Hollywood was beginning to dominate other regions where films were popular, especially Europe. As a medium, movies had a growing influence on everyday life. People copied almost everything major movie stars wore, said, and did — even their hairstyles and mannerisms.

Comedy stars of the time included Harold Lloyd (1893–1971). In Safety Last (1923), he climbs a skyscraper for his girlfriend. Lloyd's movies were full of amazing stunts.

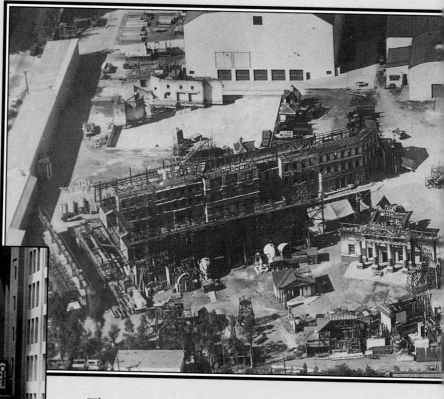

The movie Metropolis (1926), by German director Fritz Lang, was about robotlike workers in a factory of the future. Its weird scenes were influenced by recent artistic trends, even in poetry and furniture design.

FACT OR FICTION?

At first, there were worries that moviegoers would confuse screen events with daily reality, but these fears were unfounded, and cinema flourished. Comedy was king, led by Charlie Chaplin in *The Kid* (1921) and *The Gold Rush* (1925). Different genres, or kinds, of films emerged. Among them were American adventures in the Wild West, such as *The Covered Wagon* (1923); religious epics, such as *The Ten Commandments* (1923); and war stories, such as *The Big Parade* (1925).

ARTISTIC EXPRESSION

European films were less concerned with realism and more concerned with art and impressions. In the huge, newly-formed nation of the USSR, Sergei Eisenstein's *Battleship Potemkin* (1925) showed many innocent people dying during the Russian revolution.

The Covered Wagon shows a wagon train of heroic pioneers crossing the American West. Movies shaped people's views of U. S. history, although not always accurately.

Huge film companies, called studios, were in cutthroat competition to make the most successful films. They built massive moviemaking centers around Los Angeles, California, and each studio had its group of stars.

FILMING REAL LIFE

Documentaries record real life, as it happens, without interference from filmmakers. The idea began in 1921 with *Nanook of the North*, a 57-minute film by Robert Flaherty about the life of an Inuit (then called Eskimo) family. Documentaries quickly became a popular movie genre. Today, most documentary films are shown on television.

Tragically, Nanook died soon after the film was made.

YOU AIN'T HEARD NOTHING

At first, movies were silent, although some had music in the background, usually played by a pianist, or other live musicians, or from a recording. No sound, however, came directly from the action happening on the screen — until 1927.

Lights of New York (1928), starring Helene Costello and Cullen Landis, is the story of a dancer who gets mixed up with big-time criminals. This film was not only an early example of the gangster movie but also the first film with a full-length sound track.

The "talkies" led to a 1930s boom in musicals. The Wizard of Oz (1939) won an Academy Award for the song "Over the Rainbow." It was also one of the first Technicolor movies.

OVERNIGHT SENSATION

Audiences were astonished when, at one point in *The Jazz Singer*, the star, singer-actor Al Jolson, said, "You ain't seen nothing yet!" The words seemed to come directly from his lips. *The Jazz Singer*, produced in 1927 by Warner Brothers studio, was partly silent but had four musical sequences and some spoken lines. The sounds came from a disk recording that was precisely linked to the film projector. The name "talkies" was given to films with sound locked into, or synchronized with, screen action.

Movie stars became objects of fan worship. Adoring followers stood in lines for hours, hoping to catch a glimpse of their heroes.

NO "SQUEAKIES"

Welford Beaton, movie critic and editor of the Hollywood-based weekly *The Film Spectator*, wrote, "If I were an actor with a squeaky voice, I would worry." He was right! Within a year of *The Jazz Singer*'s release, silent movies were almost dead, and stars had to have attractive voices as well as acting skills. As the difficulties of recording sound tracks took the filmmaking focus away from the visual, audiences complained that "motion pictures" had little motion and few interesting pictures.

FILMING THE NEWS

Before television became widespread, people could see the news at the cinema. Important events were filmed, then shown as newsreels, which were usually short features before main movies. Newsreels often became raw material for filmmakers who made famous events into motion pictures.

Movie cameras joined the rows of newspaper photographers who lined up to record important events on film.

DANCERS AND GANGSTERS

In the 1930s, Hollywood's seemingly endless list of famous stars included Greta Garbo, Mae West, Marlene Dietrich, Bette Davis, Cary Grant, Gary Cooper, and Clark Gable. Fred Astaire and Ginger Rogers danced "cheek to cheek" in *Top Hat* (1935). James Cagney was *The Public Enemy* (1931) in a new style of film, the gangster movie.

There were few special effects in the films of the 1930s. Even the roaring lion that was the symbol of MGM studio was filmed "live."

SOUNDS OF MUSIC

Recorded sound had gained popularity since the invention of mass-produced, flat disks by Emile Berliner in 1901. Sales of disks rose steadily as more people bought gramophones — the machines to play them on.

A radio factory in 1933

Sounds were coded on a gramophone disk as a wavy groove that spiraled into the center. Most recordings lasted about five minutes.

This 1935 movie projector could play sound tracks recorded either on disks or as patterns of light alongside the movie images.

22

During the first few years of the "talkies," a movie's sound track was on a gramophone-style disk. The disk was checked under a microscope for flaws and other problems.

NOT JUST MUSIC

By the 1920s, sound recordings were more than just songs and music. They contained speeches, poetry, plays, and dramas, too. In the 1930s, however, sales of disks fell off rapidly. Radio was the main reason. A radio set provided all types of sounds for only the cost of the receiver.

TUMBLING PRICES

The prices of gramophones, radios, and similar sound equipment began to fall during the 1920s, partly as a result of mass production on assembly lines. This manufacturing method was invented in 1913 by the Ford Motor Company, to make cars. Radio broadcasting companies encouraged sales of sound equipment so more people would be influenced by sound media.

The first "tape" recorders actually used wires to store sound as magnetic patches. Flexible tape with a thin iron coating was developed in 1936.

SOUND TRACKS

By 1930, all movies had sound tracks. Why pay for a disk recording of songs, when you could hear them — and see them performed — at the cinema? The recorded music industry shifted to working on musical films, using singing stars of the silver screen. Recordings of orchestras, classical music, and operas, however, still sold well. These kinds of works were not featured in movies or on the radio nearly as often as other types of music.

GOING ELECTRIC

Advancements in recorded sound technology were linked to radio and films. At first, movie audiences had to sit near gramophone-style sound horns as they watched the screen. Later, engineers began to use electricity to increase, or amplify, the sound. The electromagnetic loudspeaker, which is still used today, was developed by General Electric in the late 1920s.

23

THE MICROPHONE

The first microphones were created in about 1925. As sound waves hit a flexible sheet called a diaphragm, they make a wire coil vibrate near a magnet, producing varying electrical signals. Before microphones, performers had to cluster around a funnel-shaped horn, and most quiet sounds were lost.

— Sound waves

— Diaphragm

— Wire coil
— Magnet

— Electrical signal

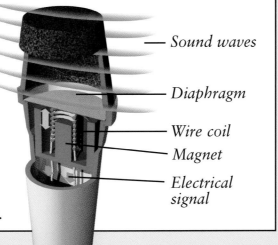

From 1931, Bell Laboratories' "Oscar" tested stereo sound. Each of Oscar's ears received slightly different sounds for better all-around realism.

PRINT WARS

When the word "tabloid" was invented in 1884, it referred to a small package containing medicine — a tablet. By 1920, "tabloid" was being used to refer to another kind of "package," containing news — the tabloid newspaper.

EASIER TO READ

Tabloids were smaller than most other newspapers, which were called broadsheets. A tabloid had big headlines, big pictures, and easy-to-read text with a focus on sensational and human-interest stories. One of the first major tabloid newspapers was London's *Daily Mirror*, founded in 1903 by Alfred Harmsworth (1865–1922), who became Viscount Northcliffe. When Northcliffe died, the paper was selling well over a million copies daily.

24

Telephones, radio, and faster printing presses meant that newspapers could report on events, such as sports contests, within an hour after an event had finished.

Northcliffe (left) was succeeded by his brother Harold (1868–1940), or Viscount Rothermere (right). The other man here (center) is another brother.

GROWING TREND

The Amalgamated Press company, owned by Viscounts Northcliffe and Rothermere, was the biggest print media group of the time, but the idea of inexpensive tabloid newspapers was spreading rapidly in both Europe and the United States. In New York, Joseph Patterson founded the *Daily News* in 1919, followed, in 1924, by Bernarr Macfadden's *Evening Graphic* and William Randolph Hearst's *Daily Mirror*.

Reporters phoned in their stories in sections, such as during halftime at a sports event, to save precious time in beating rival papers.

TOWER OF POWER

Each day, newspapers were read by millions of people, so they wielded tremendous influence in the stories they covered and the opinions they expressed. Because they could not compete with the speed of radio in first announcing, or "breaking," a story, many newspapers turned to more in-depth, detailed analyses of events, looking behind the news. Their editorial columns, feature articles, and letters enabled a variety of people to express differing viewpoints. The *New York Times*, founded in 1851, became the most respected daily newspaper in the United States.

The prestigious offices of the New York Times *(1924)*

JAZZ JOURNALISM

A tabloid's small size was an important benefit. On crowded buses and trains, people could read it more easily than the larger-format broadsheets. The short, snappy, drama-packed reporting style, with lots of pictures, became known as "jazz journalism." Broadsheets, with their longer, in-depth reports, complained that tabloids did not take world events seriously. It was tabloids, however, that helped maintain the popularity of newspapers in the face of the radio boom.

Many reporters and photographers were from press agencies. They gathered news and took pictures, then sold them to the newspapers.

LIFE AND TIME

During the 1920s, several new types of magazines began to change the style of publishing. Most of them originated in the United States, then spread to Europe. These publications included *Time*, *Life*, and *Reader's Digest*.

During the 1930s, city newsstands were swamped with new magazines and journals. Many were designed for people traveling to and from work.

Henry Luce (1898–1967) adapted the format of Time *magazine as a radio program and, then, as a film series called* The March of Time.

This issue of Life *was the first one Luce published. The focus of the October 1936 issue of* Fortune *was photography.*

NOVEMBER 23, 1936   10 CENTS

FOR BUSY READERS

The leading publisher behind the new style of magazines was Henry Luce. With his colleague Briton Hadden, Luce started *Time* in 1923. *Time* was a weekly news summary, written for the more educated public. For busy readers, its contents were arranged in easy-to-follow sections, and it had many high-quality pictures. Even after the United States entered the Depression, *Time* was a huge success, so, in 1930, Luce started *Fortune* magazine. *Life* magazine, which followed in 1936, became the biggest seller of all weekly picture magazines.

PHOTOJOURNALISM

Life had been a satire-based periodical since 1883. Luce bought it in 1935 and changed it to be the magazine for readers who wanted "to see life, to see the world, to eyewitness great events." The news was told mainly with photographs that had explanatory captions, a medium known as photojournalism. Luce's political views were very conservative and very anticommunist. He used his publications, his editor-in-chief position, and his money to influence the public and to affect the U. S. government's views on communist nations.

These Penguin Books are eight of the first ten paperbacks. With paperbacks, books were suddenly inexpensive enough for almost anyone to buy.

A NOVEL IDEA

In 1935, British publisher Allen Lane started a new trend in books — paperbacks. At the time, most books were hardbacks, which were expensive to buy and often valued more for their leather covers and quality bindings than for their contents. Paperbacks were inexpensive, read-anywhere, throwaway novels — and an instant success.

The 1930s trend for illustrated magazines spread to many countries. This issue of the French L'Illustré *is from 1932.*

HOW SMALL BECAME HUGE

Former book salesman DeWitt Wallace and his wife, Lila Acheson, started *Reader's Digest*, in the United States, in 1920. Their approach was to take news, features, and articles that had been printed elsewhere and make them into condensed summaries, or "digests." *Reader's Digest* was designed for people who wanted to read a variety of topics quickly, yet still find important information. It was small enough in size to fit in a coat pocket, but it grew to be one of the world's most successful publications.

DeWitt (1889–1981) and Lila (1889–1984) Wallace

THE READER'S DIGEST

31 ARTICLES EACH MONTH FROM LEAD-ING MAGAZINES, EACH ARTICLE OF ENDURING VALUE AND INTEREST, IN CONDENSED AND PERMANENT FORM.

January, 1920

WORLD AT WAR

As the 1930s progressed, the media had no shortage of events to report. Wars and other conflicts broke out in many parts of the world. Then came the news that many people dreaded. Another World War had begun.

NAZI THREAT

Adolf Hitler became Germany's leader in 1933. As his Nazi movement gained strength, Hitler built up Germany's military forces. Nations such as France, Britain, and the United States remained neutral, trying to avoid an all-out war. Then, in 1938, German forces invaded Austria. As American radio reporter Edward Murrow (1908–1965) gave a somber account of Hitler's arrival in Vienna, Austria's capital, millions of listeners realized, for the first time, that the Nazi campaign was an urgent threat to world peace.

Many European children were sent away from unsafe areas. Newspapers helped them stay in touch with home.

Edward Murrow (right), shown here with colleague William Shirer, was the leading war correspondent of his time. His reports were concise and accurate, and they managed to convey the horror of battle.

British prime minister Neville Chamberlain is waving an agreement from Adolf Hitler to stop military activity in Europe. Within a year after this photograph, World War II had begun.

THE PROPAGANDA WAR

Compared to World War I, the media's reporting of World War II was generally more open, accurate, and faster. Radio links could flash news, both words and pictures, across continents in seconds. Nations listened to each other's programs. Some even broadcasted directly to the enemy. Listeners were told that their country was not fighting a just cause and could never win the war, so the best choice was immediate surrender. This type of selective, biased information, produced specially to advance or propagate a cause, is known as propaganda — and it flourishes in wartime.

This poster by Pierre Mail portrays the suffering of left-wing activists under right-wing Fascists during the Spanish Civil War (1936–1939).

CONFLICT IN THE EAST

World War II quickly spread to East Asia. Since the late 1920s, Japanese military officers had been seizing senior government positions. They used newspapers, radio, movies, and other media to praise Japan's great military history. People were told that Japan would soon rise again as a major world power. As a result, public support for conflict increased. In 1937, Japan attacked China. In 1940, the Japanese signed military agreements with Germany and Italy, and the war raged.

Chinese posters honored their glorious army.

TIME LINE

	WORLD EVENTS	HEADLINES	MEDIA EVENTS	TECHNOLOGY	THE ARTS
1920	•U.S.: women get vote	•Joan of Arc is canonized to sainthood	•Reader's Digest magazine begins	•UK: Marconi makes short-wave radio connection	•Edith Wharton: The Age of Innocence
1921	•Chinese communist party founded	•France: tuberculosis vaccine developed	•Baseball World Series heard live on radio	•Baird works on scanning disk TV system	•Rudolph Valentino stars in The Sheik
1922	•Russia becomes USSR	•Formation of Irish Free State starts civil war	•New York radio station WEAF begins commercials	•Experimental car radio is first portable radio	•F. W. Murnau: Nosferatu (early horror film)
1923	•Italy: Mussolini seizes power	•Japan: earthquake kills 200,000, injures 800,000	•Time magazine founded by Luce and Hadden	•Zworykin works on all-electronic TV system	•De Mille: The Ten Commandments
1924	•Britain: first Labour government elected	•U.S.: Woodrow Wilson dies •USSR: Lenin dies	•Evening Graphic and U.S. Daily Mirror founded	•Photos transmitted by radio across Atlantic	•George Gershwin: Rhapsody in Blue
1925	•Albania gains independence	•U.S.: Coolidge becomes president	•Harold Ross founds The New Yorker magazine	•Vitaphone sound-on-disk film system created	•Paris: first Surrealist painting exhibition
1926	•Britain: General Strike •Poland: military takeover	•U.S.: Goddard launches first liquid fuel rocket	•U.S.: NBC broadcasting network formed	•Baird transmits first TV images by radio waves	•Fritz Lang: Metropolis
1927	•Russia: Stalin vs. Trotsky	•Lindbergh makes nonstop solo transatlantic flight	•U.S.: CBS broadcasting network formed	•Philo Farnsworth builds complete electronic TV	•First successful "talkie": The Jazz Singer
1928	•U.S.: Hoover elected president	•Earhart is first woman to fly across Atlantic	•Mickey Mouse introduced in Steamboat Willie	•First all-sound-track movies introduced	•Walt Disney: first Mickey Mouse cartoon
1929	•South Africa: Apartheid begins	•U.S.: Wall Street Crash, Depression begins	•Amos 'n' Andy radio shows begin	•Baird begins daily TV test broadcasts for BBC	•New York: Museum of Modern Art founded
1930	•Japan: Prime Minister Hamaguchi assassinated	•India: Ghandi leads protest marches	•Fortune magazine started by Henry Luce	•U.S.: NBC sets up TV transmitter in New York	•Noel Coward: Private Lives
1931	•Japanese army occupies Chinese Manchuria	•U.S.: Empire State Building completed	•Electronic TV broadcasts in Los Angeles & Moscow	•Bell Labs experiment with stereo recording	•Bela Lugosi stars in Dracula
1932	•France: President Doumer assassinated	•U.S.: Franklin Roosevelt elected president	•Walter Winchell's radio show begins	•Movie Napoleon has stereophonic sound	•Aldous Huxley: Brave New World
1933	•Hitler in power as Chancellor of Germany	•U.S.: prohibition repealed	•King Kong begins use of special effects in movies	•Edwin Armstrong develops FM radio	•Greta Garbo stars in Queen Christina
1934	•China: Mao Tse-tung leads Long March	•USSR enters League of Nations	•Associated Press starts wirephoto service	•Cinemas start using large loudspeakers	•Henry Miller: Tropic of Cancer
1935	•Italy invades Abyssinia (Ethiopia)	•Persia becomes Iran	•Life magazine begins limited test publications	•Technicolor developed for movies	•Benny Goodman called "King of Swing"
1936	•Spanish Civil War begins	•Germany: Olympic Games held in Berlin	•UK: BBC begins regular TV broadcasts	•Flexible magnetic tape created for sound recording	•Penguin launches paperback books
1937	•Japan attacks China	•U.S.: Hindenberg airship explodes near New York	•Radio pioneer Guglielmo Marconi dies	•Chester Carlson invents Xerography photocopier	•Disney: Snow White (first full-length animation)
1938	•Germany invades Austria	•U.S.: War of the Worlds on radio causes panic	•Radio sets in U.S. number 50 million	•Baird demonstrates live color TV	•First Superman comic strip •Wilder: Our Town
1939	•Spanish Civil War ends •World War II begins	•U.S.: New York World's Fair opens	•U.S.: FDR makes first presidential TV broadcast	•Marvin Camras invents wire sound recorder	•The Wizard of Oz (filmed in Technicolor)

GLOSSARY

cathode-ray tube: a type of vacuum tube, such as the picture tube of a television set, in which a beam of electrons "paints" pictures and other information with spots of light across a fluorescent screen.

commentator: a person who discusses, as well as reports, news on radio or television.

diaphragm: a thin, flexible partition in a microphone or loudspeaker, which vibrates easily when hit by sound waves, producing electrical signals.

modulated: adjusted a radio wave or a light wave to either a particular height or a certain frequency, forming a pattern or code that conveys information.

photocell: short for photoelectric cell, a device with electrical properties that are altered by light.

photojournalism: the technique of presenting news using mostly photographs with captions, rather than full text with only a few photographs.

propaganda: information that is often false and is spread for the specific purpose of either helping or hurting a particular cause.

satire: a style of wit or humor that makes fun of human faults and weaknesses in a nasty, biting way.

sound track: the area on a film or a videotape that carries recorded sound.

tabloid: a newspaper with a page size that is smaller than a broadsheet's but larger than a magazine's; a style of journalism that features large headlines, lots of pictures, and easy-to-read text, usually written in a sensational style.

transmitter: a device that sends out electronic signals, either over a wire or in radio waves.

triode valves: vacuum tubes that contain three small metal plates, called electrodes, which strengthen weak electrical signals to control much larger currents.

MORE BOOKS TO READ

Books and Newspapers. Communication Close-Up (series). Ian Graham (Raintree Steck-Vaughn)

Discovery Kit: Build Your Own FM Radio. Conn McQuinn (Running Press)

Eyewitness: Film. Richard Platt (DK Publishing)

Faces of Time: *75 Years of* Time *Magazine Cover Portraits.* Frederick Voss, editor (Bulfinch Press)

Guglielmo Marconi: Radio Pioneer. Giants of Science (series). Beverley Birch (Blackbirch Marketing)

John Logie Baird. Groundbreakers (series). Struan Reid (Heinemann)

The Nazi Olympics: Berlin 1936. Susan D. Bachrach (Little, Brown & Company)

Phonograph: Sound on Disk. The Encyclopedia of Discovery and Invention (series). Bradley Steffens (Gale Group)

Sounds in the Air: The Golden Age of Radio. Norman H. Finkelstein (iUniverse.com)

TV's Forgotten Hero: The Story of Philo Farnsworth. Stephanie Sammartino McPherson (Carolrhoda Books)

Who Threw That Pie? The Birth of Movie Comedy. Robert M. Quackenbush (Albert Whitman)

WEB SITES

Guglielmo Marconi 1874–1937. *www.pbs.org/wgbh/aso/databank/entries/btmarc.html*

How I Filmed *Nanook of the North.* *www.cinemaweb.com/silentfilm/bookshelf/23_rf1_2.htm*

KDKA AM 1020: Timeline. *www.kdkaradio.com/timeline.html*

Logie Baird's Television Apparatus. *www.fathom.com/feature/122245*

Due to the dynamic nature of the Internet, some web sites stay current longer than others. To find additional web sites, use a reliable search engine with one or more of the following keywords: *1936 Olympics, crystal radio set, gramophone, Edward Murrow, newspapers, radio, silent films, talkies, telegraphy, television,* and *Walter Winchell.*

INDEX